THE LAST CHAPTER, THE FIRST PAGE

EMBRACING RETIREMENT: TRANSFORMING YOUR GOLDEN YEARS WITH RESILIENCE

S.SANDEEP

Dedicated to My Beloved Family

In loving memory of my Late Parents- Mrs. Urmila & Dr. P.R. Shrivastava

My Wife - Deepti, Daughter - Priyal & Son - Prakher

&

My Sisters - Rachna, Ranjana,Roopam & Rinku

In the warmth of your memories and the love we continue to share, I find solace and strength.

Each of you has been a guiding light in my life, shaping my values and inspiring me to reach for the stars.

This tribute is a testament to the lasting impact of family bonds and the legacy of love that lives on.

Thank you for being my eternal source of love and inspiration.

Contents

Foreword

Dr. Vedprakash Mishra
Pro-Chancellor-cum-Chief Advisor
Datta Meghe Institute of Higher
Education & Research
(Deemed to be University)

Date : 23.04.2025

Life is a saga the contours and colors of which become vivid in terms of the dimensions in which the life is lived. Realistically speaking life turns out to be a tragedy to those whothink it but a genuine comedy to all those who live it.

As such, the real essence turns outto be that life has to be 'lived' not in the name of 'living it' but in the true essence of availing it to its hilt in order to enrich it not just with joys, pleasures, stimulations, and titillations, but with bliss inter alia the absolute bliss.

The material question is can it be made blissful realistically and in all 360 degrees. The emphatic answer to the same is a subtle 'Yes'. The Art and Science therefore, of making ones life blissful totally lies in the material reality that it has to be lived with 'passion and purpose in unison'.

Life is lived in phases by one and all in as much as each life has its 'formative phase', 'creative phase', and 'a terminal phase'.

Nobody has been immune from the same ever since antiquity. Hence the saga of a blissful life lies in ensuring every phase of it is plagued by absolute bliss. No corner, no contour should remain untouched turns out to be the cardinal key.

It is true that the formative phase with bubbling youth does not call for much, the creative phase with passion, pursuance, perseverance, devotion, dedication, discipline, courage, conviction and commitment invariably makes it worthwhile, joyous and blissful as a whole.

By and large it can be put across in the form of a thumb rule that the formative and creative phase of life do not call for critical discerning in the context of calculative analytics in order to get them enriched and ornamented as the task is reasonably handy, specially because it is occupied in its entirety with demonstrable spectrum of achievements, accolades, recognitions, visibility and also placement at positions of power, authority including accrual of glory and impact which have their not only soothing effect but also the demonstrative essence of achievements, attainments and accomplishments as well.

The some and substance of the creative phase of life is its domination by 'Ascendency' in tangible and measurable way which makes it totally blissful. But as the dictum goes that every 'ascendency' has to meet with its decline and resultant 'descendancy' as a natural corollary and therefore, terminal phase of life which in its routine parlance can be said to be 'post retirement life' with descendancy in a roundabout manner as a rule dominating it, the search for joy, pleasure turning out to be dim and a matter of rarity, the same getting blissful looks like a near impossibility.

But then here is a valuable treatise which has been put by the author Dr. Sandeep Shrivastava in a rare inimitable style in this Book has unearthed a treasure inter alia a gold mine which has brought out a subtle pathway treading upon which would not only make and transform the post retirement life worth living, but also engulfing it by nothing else than absolute bliss.

The depiction in the four chapters beautifully syntaxed, appropriately worded, analytically described and emphatically discerned have emphatically brought out a way forward which is handy, doable and consequential in terms of one feeling 'tired' of life in the domain of uselessness and nothingness would stand transformed to getting 'retyred' is the real 'mantra', which can create not just a ripple but ensure a whole ocean of bliss and bliss alone handily standing out at the doorsteps with open arms to embrace and make the last terminal phase of life not only livable but laudably worthwhile.

It is not just an attempt by the author to bring out a casual fill-up of the sense of nothingness and or vacuum but a subtle indicative pathway and doable modalities which end up in desired transformation evoking unparalleled satisfaction in terms of living the said phase of life once again allover with newer passion, but not with passivity with newer vigor but not with aggressive and imposing vitality but pursuing it with the sole purpose of adding 'meaning' to it beyond the realm of any sense of achievement or accomplishment but exclusively relishing the lap of 'self-actualization' in its truest sensse and purest essence.

As such, this unique, unparalleled and creative work of the author embodied in this book is not just a worthwhile attempt in the much desired domain and direction but has resulted in bringing out a subtlety of purpose and meaning in hitherto conceived as 'meaningless' and without any focus and purpose.

I find my words at bay to compliment the author for this rare novelty which he has penned rather crafted diligently with passion and involvement in a manner which is not just probing depth but it is unfathoming the deepest to bring out the craft which is need of the hour to evoke a new succor and lease of much needed vibrance in existing domain of disillusionment, despondence, depression, so as to end this script of life by its transformation into a ' Scripture' as a whole in its truest sense making the entire spectrum of life plagued by bliss, bliss and bliss alone including nothing else but 'Absolute bliss'.

**Professor of Excellence, Professor of Eminence,
Professor Emeritus and Distinguished Professor**
Dr. Vedprakash Mishra
**Dr. B. C. Roy National Awardee,
D.Sc. (Honoris Causa) by Seven Universities**
Secretary General, International Council of Global Network for Medical, Health Professions & Bioethics Education,
President, Association of Medical Educators of India (AMEI)
International Co-Chair Global Network of Medical and Health Professions Education Melbourne Australia
Head of the Medical and Health Professions Schools of the Indian program of the ICB-UNESCO Chair
Chairperson, National Task Force on Medical Education constituted by NAMS, Government of India
National Head of the Academic Programme of Indian Programme UNESCO Chair in Bio-Ethics Haifa & Member of the
International Committee for Bioethics for Asia Pacific Region

Chief Advisor to Hon'ble Chancellor and Krishna Institute of Medical Sciences (Deemed to be University), Karad

Dean, Academic and Accreditation Board, National Indian Medical Association, New Delhi
Honorary Professor, Indian Medical Association
Honorary Director, Centre for Health Sciences Education Policy and Planning, DMIHER (DU), Nagpur
Former Pro-Chancellor, Datta Meghe Institute of Higher Education & Research (Deemed to be University), Nagpur
Former Vice Chancellor, Datta Meghe Institute of Medical Sciences (Deemed University), Nagpur
Former Chairman, Postgraduate Medical Education Committee, Medical Council of India, New Delhi
Former Chairman, Academic Council, Medical Council of India, New Delhi

FOREWORD

Preface

S.Sandeep

Welcome.

This is more than just a book.

It's an invitation—to pause, reflect, and gently unpack the layers of a life that has seen many seasons. Retirement, the empty nest, and the quiet moments that follow are not the end of the story. In fact, they offer a new beginning—one where you finally have the space to turn inward, to ask yourself questions that may have waited decades for your attention.

Who am I now, without the role of a busy professional or a full-time parent?

What gives my day meaning, now that the to-do lists have thinned?

How do I fill the quiet spaces without feeling lost in them?

These aren't always easy questions. But they're beautiful ones. And this workbook was created to help you explore them—not with pressure or urgency, but with care, curiosity, and a sense of companionship.

Each section offers space to write, to wonder, and to simply *be*. There's no right or wrong way to go through these pages. You may want to read them all at once, or you might return to them over days or weeks—like a favorite chair that's always waiting for you.

The chapters ahead gently touch upon life's transitions:
– The shift from doing to being
– The challenge of redefining identity after decades of responsibility
– The emotional terrain of loneliness, and how to navigate it with grace
– The joy of rediscovering passions, purpose, and peace

This is your time. You've earned it.

So breathe deeply. Pick up your pen. Let your story unfold in your own handwriting.

You're not alone. Let's begin—together.

This book has 4 chapters

Chapter 1: A fore-story about a typical retirement and post-retirement challenges faced .

Chapter 2 :The concepts for building resilience- I. General II. Key and III. Vital ,interwoven with some exercises.

Chapter 3: A workbook on important concepts of resilience as discussed and keep updating them regularly.

Chapter 4: To do tips for emotional strength, physical strength , nutrition and an ideal daily routine.

I hope this help to navigate another very important phase of life , with retirement around.

Best wishes for a pleasant life ahead.

Dr. Sandeep Shrivastava,

23rd April 2025

Executive Director, International
Professor -Orthopaedics, J.N.Medical College ,Wardha
Chief Scintific Officer, DMIHER,DU
Hon. Director Centre for Advance Joint Replacement Centre
Hon. Director Centre for Regenrative Medicine
Hon. Advisor Clinical Reserach Division.
Former DEAN ,J.N.Medical College Wardha
Former Chief Executive Officer , Hospitals (DMIHER ,DU

Acknowledgements

As I stepped into the golden chapter of my life, a quiet yet persistent voice within urged me to pause, reflect, and prepare more mindfully for the journey ahead.

It was during this time that Shrikrishna , my trusted Chartered Accountant , gently steered my attention toward financial clarity and stability. His encouragement became the seed from which this book began to grow. With technology as a reassuring companion, what once felt overwhelming became a manageable, even meaningful, endeavour.

This book is a heartfelt tribute to those who stood by me with unwavering faith and love. My deepest gratitude goes to my dearest family—**Deepti, Priyal, and Prakher**—whose quiet presence, encouragement, and belief in me became my guiding light. Your love has been the wind beneath my wings.

To my beloved sisters—**Rachna, Ranjana, Roopam, and Rinku**—and their families, thank you for your boundless support and affection. You reminded me of the strength that lies in familial bonds and the comfort of shared roots.

I am especially thankful to my colleagues whose wisdom and camaraderie enriched this journey. **Mr. Shrikrishna Dinkar Ambarkar**, once again, for highlighting the significance of financial mindfulness in these years of transition. **Dr. Roma Morghade (Sarnaik)** whose thoughtful perspectives as a lifestyle consultant added depth and dimension to this work. And to my departmental peers, walking parallel paths—thank you for the shared understanding and insights.

A special note of reverence goes to **Dr. Ved Prakash Mishra**—a beacon of wisdom in my life for over two decades. His gracious acceptance to pen the foreword, and doing so with profound thoughtfulness within just 24 hours, is a testament to his brilliance and generosity of spirit. I am deeply honored and forever grateful.

To the dedicated team at **Notion Press**, thank you for bringing this vision to life with such grace and professionalism.

This book is my humble offering to all those who seek solace, clarity, and meaning in the second act of life. May it be a comforting hand to hold and a gentle nudge toward rediscovering purpose and peace.

Prologue

Last Chapter, First Page
A gentle, empowering guide to embracing retirement and rediscovering purpose.
What happens when the roles we've held for decades begin to fade?

In this moving blend of story and self-help, follow Arjun—a seasoned doctor—as he navigates retirement, an empty home, and the loss of his beloved wife. With wisdom drawn from friendship and the *Bhagavad Gita*, Arjun's journey becomes a roadmap for anyone facing life's quiet, later transitions.
Packed with reflective exercises, practical advice on financial and emotional resilience, and tips for living meaningfully,
Last Chapter, First Page is more than a book—it's a compassionate companion for your golden years.

1

CHAPTER 1 :

A story of Golden year

Scene 1: Retirement Day

Dr. Arjun Malhotra stood on the hospital dais, his white coat folded over his arm like a soldier laying down arms after a long, hard-fought battle. The applause echoed off the walls—loud, thunderous, and overwhelming—but to him, it sounded distant, as if he were underwater. His students spoke of his legacy, his colleagues offered heartfelt gratitude, and garlands hung heavy around his neck. Yet inside, a quiet fear brewed: "Who am I without this? What becomes of a healer when there are no more wounds to mend?"

"Meera, his wife of thirty-five years, stood by the door, her eyes soft with understanding. Her calm demeanor masked a steely resolve, one that had carried them through decades of triumphs and struggles.

She clapped politely but never took her eyes off him.

She knew this moment was bittersweet for him.

She had always known. The world saw a celebrated doctor, but she saw the cracks—the exhaustion, the self-doubt, the quiet man who feared the silence that was about to engulf his life."

Later that evening, as they sat together in their unusually silent bungalow, a heavy air of introspection enveloped Arjun and Meera. Arjun's gaze lingered on his untouched plate, the weight of realization settling upon him like a shroud. "It's strange, Meera. All these years, I've been running on a clock. Every moment had a purpose. And now... it feels like the clock has stopped," he confessed, his voice filled with a mix of longing and uncertainty.

Meera, acutely aware of the profound shift in their lives, reached out across the table, her touch imbued with unspoken strength and resolve. "Arjun, clocks don't stop. They just reset. This isn't the end. It's the beginning of a new time," she declared, her words cutting through the silence like a beacon of hope in the darkness.

Attempting to ease the heaviness of the moment with a touch of warmth, Meera lovingly reminisced, "Remember our cozy dinners by the fireplace? This new chapter is like that—a chance to embrace the warmth of togetherness and create new memories in the flickering lights of our shared love."

Their laughter rang out, a fragile melody in the midst of the storm of emotions swirling around them.

Yet beneath the facade of humor, the gravity of the moment loomed large. Meera's teasing smile masked a deep-seated concern for Arjun. She understood that retirement wasn't just a pause—it was a profound reinvention, a daunting journey into the unknown where the familiar rhythms of life had been replaced by uncharted territories of change and transformation.

As tears glistened in Meera's eyes, reflecting the unspoken emotions that words could not convey, she whispered softly, "Our love has weathered every storm, Arjun. In this new chapter, let's find solace in each other's embrace and rewrite the story of our lives with courage and unwavering faith." In that moment, the depth of their bond and the fragility of human resilience intertwined, painting a portrait of love that resonated with the echoes of eternity.

Scene 2: The Financial Talk

The next morning, as the gentle sunlight kissed the garden with warmth, Meera and Arjun sat together, savoring the comforting aroma of chai that enveloped them. Birds chirped melodiously, adding a serene backdrop to the conversation that was about to unfold.

Meera gazed at Arjun with a mixture of concern and determination, breaking the silence that had lingered between them for years. "Arjun, now that you've retired, have you thought about how we're going to manage things?" Her words hung in the air, heavy with unspoken truths and the weight of responsibility.

Arjun furrowed his brow, a hint of worry creasing his features as he lowered his cup, the clink of porcelain echoing softly. "We've always been careful with money, Meera. I thought we were fine," he responded, his voice tinged with uncertainty.

> "*Meera's smile was like a gentle embrace, radiating warmth and understanding. "We are fine, Arjun. But retirement isn't just about having enough money—it's about planning how to use it wisely so we're not worried. You know how much I cherish our little home and the garden, but we need to consider healthcare, emergencies, and even the simple joys like traveling or exploring new hobbies."*"

Leaning forward, her eyes brimming with unwavering determination, Meera's voice was a perfect balance of firmness and kindness. "I don't want us to live with anxiety in our golden years. Let's make a plan—together," she urged, bridging the gap between uncertainty and hope with her unwavering support and love.

As Arjun met Meera's gaze, a sense of relief washed over him, knowing that they were in this together. The garden around them seemed to echo their shared resolve, blooming with the promise of a future filled with careful planning, shared dreams, and the unbreakable bond that held them close.

Scene 3: Making a Plan

That weekend, as the sunlight filtered through the curtains, casting a warm glow over the room, Meera sat at the table with a notebook and a calculator, deep in thought as she meticulously planned the family's finances. Arjun watched her with a mix of admiration and fondness, his mind drifting to a nostalgic memory from their early years of marriage.

"Alright, my love," Meera playfully teased, her eyes gleaming with determination, "let's organize our budget for the family. First, we'll list our essential expenses—like household bills, groceries, and insurance. Then, we'll set aside funds for unexpected events and savings. And, of course, we must allocate a budget for those special family occasions, like the dream vacation we've always talked about."

Arjun couldn't help but smile at Meera's attention to detail and their shared dreams. "You've always had a way with numbers, haven't you?" he remarked, a touch of nostalgia coloring his words.

"That's the secret to keeping our family strong and our dreams alive," Meera replied with a gentle smile, her love for her family shining brightly.

As they delved into the financial planning, a memory surfaced in Arjun's mind—a time when a sudden financial crisis had tested their relationship and forced them to lean on each other for support during the early years of their marriage.

"Do you remember when we faced that unexpected financial challenge during Rishi's birth?" Arjun's voice was soft, carrying a hint of emotion as he recalled the trying time.

Meera's expression softened, her gaze meeting Arjun's with understanding. "I do. It was a difficult period, but it brought us closer together and taught us the importance of financial preparedness in all circumstances. It's moments like those that remind us of the strength of our bond and the importance of planning for the future, no matter what life may bring."

Their conversation took on a deeper meaning as they reflected on the challenges they had overcome together and the resilience of their family unit. In that moment, amidst the calculations and projections, the true essence of their partnership shone through—the unwavering love, support, and shared commitment to a future filled with security, dreams, and the enduring bond that defined their family's journey together.

Scene 4: Retirement – A New Beginning

In the late afternoon, as the sun cast a warm, golden hue across the room, Meera reached for Arjun's hand. Her touch was a gentle reassurance, igniting a spark of warmth within him. Her voice, like a soothing melody, carried a sense of unwavering certainty and love. "Arjun, this isn't an end. It's a rare chance—a rebirth. You've spent your life mending bones and easing pain. Now it's time to rediscover yourself. Let's travel. Let's paint new landscapes, not just on canvas, but in our lives," Meera's words resonated with a hint of excitement and anticipation, painting a vision of shared adventures and boundless possibilities.Her words, filled with passion and love, cut through the haze of uncertainty clouding his mind. She wasn't just speaking of trips or hobbies; she was inviting him into a shared vision—one alive with laughter, discovery, and the quiet joy of togetherness

"We could finally see the Himalayas at sunrise, or start that health initiative in the village. Retirement doesn't have to mean retreat—it can be redemption. A way to serve in a different, deeper way," Meera's vision painted a vivid picture of a future brimming with purpose and fulfillment.As Meera's words washed over him, her eyes sparkling in the soft afternoon light, Arjun felt a wave of peace wash over him. Her unwavering faith in him and their shared future sparked something long dormant within him—a flicker of curiosity, a pulse of hope.

Maybe this chapter wouldn't be a slow fade—but a vibrant bloom, rich with new experiences and shared dreams. As Meera spoke, her unwavering gaze reflecting the gentle afternoon glow, Arjun realized that it wasn't about filling time; it was about creating meaning and embracing the journey ahead.

In a rare moment of quietude, husband and wife sat in content companionship, with nothing but the softly ticking clock and the shared glow of the late afternoon sun to fill the room. The absence of words was a comfort, a silent reminder of the depth of their connection and the peace found in each other's presence. As they sat in serene stillness, the world outside faded away, leaving only the gentle rustle of leaves and the beating of their intertwined hearts to break the peaceful silence, enveloping them in a moment of blissful togetherness.

Scene 5 : A Flicker of Temptation

Still, the transformation wasn't immediate. Doubt lingered.

Arjun, though inspired, remained tethered to caution. His memories—fractured stories of patients, of healing and heartbreak—called to him. He wondered if they could live again on the page.

With Meera's gentle prodding, he signed up for a local creative writing workshop. It was led by Sanya, a magnetic novelist whose presence seemed to crackle with promise.

Sanya urged her students to mine their scars for truth.
"Write what you ache to say," she told him, locking eyes during one session. "Your stories have weight. Let them breathe."

Her passion ignited something unfamiliar. In their exchanges—laced with wit and shared silences—Arjun found both exhilaration and unease. She saw him not as a retired surgeon, but as a man on the cusp of reinvention. That attention, intoxicating in its intensity, shook him.

One evening, after a particularly stirring class, Sanya suggested coffee. In the quiet corner of a dim café, she leaned in.

"You have immense potential, Arjun," she said softly. "Don't shrink from this. Let it take you somewhere new."

The air thickened. His heart pounded—not with excitement, but with the weight of conflict. Meera's laughter, their dreams, her unwavering faith—they rose within him like a tide.

> *He smiled, but it trembled. "I want to embrace the new," he said, "but not at the cost of the one who's always believed in me."*

Outside, the night had deepened, but something inside him had clarified: this new chapter would be written not just in bold choices, but in the quiet strength of fidelity, of staying true to a love that had weathered storms and still held light.

Scene 6: The Story Beneath the Silence

In the tranquility of the evening, as the neem leaves gently brushed against the window, Meera sought solace in a book, wrapped in the soft glow of the lamplight. Arjun, captivated by the serene grace of his wife, carried the weight of a challenging day in the operating career—where a young girl's fragile life teetered on the brink of loss.

Summoning his courage, Arjun's voice quivered with emotion as he recalled, "Meera, I... I had just completed a complex surgery that day, fighting to save a young girl clinging to life." Her eyes widened with empathy, reliving the intense emotions of that pivotal juncture in their intertwined journey.

With trembling hands, Arjun handed her the crumpled pages, unveiling, "I've recorded the intricate details of the surgery, uncertain of its impact. But I wanted you to be part of this profound moment." Meera accepted the pages reverently, her heart pounding with shared anxiety and hope as she immersed herself in the narrative of the life-altering operation.

As she traversed the highs and lows of the surgical saga, Arjun watched her intently, capturing every fleeting emotion etched across her face. A furrowed brow, a sigh of relief, and the hint of glistening tears mirrored the intense emotional turmoil of the life-and-death circumstances he had faced.

Upon finishing the account, Meera's eyes glistened with pride and poignant emotion. "Arjun, this is extraordinary. Your courage, expertise, and compassion resonate throughout every page. You not only preserved a life but also shared a tale of resilience and optimism."

In that poignant moment of shared triumph and connection, as Meera clasped his hand, her admiration and unwavering support stirred a profound sense of purpose and accomplishment within Arjun. It transcended beyond the realm of successful surgery; it embodied the profound impact of his actions and the transformative influence of storytelling to inspire and heal.

Acknowledging his profound calling, Arjun affirmed, "Perhaps this is my destiny—to heal not only with my hands but with the power of words." Meera's steadfast backing and encouragement fortified his resolve.

""Continue sharing your experiences, Arjun. The world awaits your narratives of bravery and compassion. I'll stand by you, championing your every endeavor," she affirmed, her words suffused with love and

unwavering faith, igniting a fervent sense of purpose and creativity within his being."

Scene 7: The Empty Nest – A Masterpiece of Resilience

The day approached with quiet insistence—Rishi was leaving for medical school. And with every zipped suitcase and folded shirt, Meera felt the ache of time catching up with her. The house that once thrummed with his laughter, his clumsy piano tunes, the scent of his midnight snacks, would soon stand still.

> *"Motherhood had been Meera's symphony—its crescendos and silences composing her days. But now, with the music softening, she stood at the edge of a new silence, unsure whether it would be emptiness or possibility."*

That evening, as the sun dipped into the horizon like a slow exhale, Meera sat beside Arjun on their veranda. The air was fragrant with chameli blossoms, but her eyes brimmed with unshed tears.

"Arjun," she whispered, "what if I'm not ready for this silence? I've mothered every corner of this house. What am I, when the boy who gave me that name walks out the door?"

Arjun reached for her hand, the same hand he'd held through births, losses, surgeries, and celebrations.

"You're still everything," he said. "You're Meera—the woman who gave our son roots and wings. And now... we dream again. Together."

She looked at him, searching for anchor in his calm.

"The nest may empty," he continued, "but our hearts can grow fuller still."

He paused, smiling softly. "I dream of hearing small feet run through this house again. Of a little girl calling you Dadi, hiding behind your saree. A little boy sneaking sweets from my study drawer."

Meera laughed through her tears, the image wrapping itself around her grief like a shawl.

"And of Rishi walking through that gate," she added, "with a kind girl by his side. One who'll light up his world like you lit up mine."

Arjun nodded. "She'll be our daughter too. Not by blood, but by love. We'll welcome her with open arms—and stories."

On the Eve of Departure

The farewell dinner was full of noise and celebration. Relatives clinked glasses, neighbors shared old memories, and Rishi—poised, nervous, excited—stood in the center of it all, caught in a moment he would remember for life.

Later, when the house fell quiet and the dishes were done, Arjun pulled his son aside.

"I want you to chase your own light, Rishi. Don't carry my shadow. Be gentle. Be curious. And don't be afraid to love deeply, whether it's your patients or your partner."

Rishi hugged him, voice thick with emotion. "I will, Dad. I promise. And when the time comes... I'll bring someone home you'll both be proud of."

"Meera, listening from the hallway, smiled—eyes glistening not just with sorrow, but with hope."

In the Days That Followed

The silence in the house no longer felt like a loss. It felt like space—sacred and waiting.

Arjun returned to his writing, pouring stories onto paper like a man finding a second wind. Meera took up sketching again, capturing forgotten dreams in charcoal and color. They hosted storytelling nights for neighborhood children, laughed over old recipes, and planned a trip to the mountains where they had once promised to grow old together.

And sometimes, late at night, Meera would whisper into the quiet, "One day, this home will be noisy again—with giggles and lullabies. One day, we'll tell bedtime stories not just as parents, but as grandparents."

"The nest was empty. But the sky—wide and welcoming—was filled with dreams still waiting to hatch."

Scene 8 : A Sudden Storm

The storm hit without warning—sudden, fierce, and unforgiving. The sky darkened in an instant, thunder roaring like a beast unleashed, lightning slicing through the clouds with violent precision. It was an ordinary morning—peaceful, quiet, almost mundane. Meera had just finished making her signature masala chai, humming softly as she moved around the kitchen, her spirit light, unaware of the chaos brewing outside.

Arjun sat at the dining table, immersed in the newspaper, the aroma of her perfume blending with the spicy warmth of the tea. For a moment, everything felt safe, familiar—until her voice broke the silence.

"Arjun," she called from the kitchen, her tone casual, almost playful. "Do you think we should repaint the living room? It's been years since—" Her words trailed off, a hint of hesitation in her voice.

Suddenly, the world seemed to tilt. The cup in her hand wobbled, trembling as if caught in a tremor of unseen forces. Then, with a heartbreaking shatter, it hit the floor, shards scattering like tiny explosions.

"Meera?" Arjun's voice sharpened, laced with rising panic. His eyes darted to her, fear flickering like lightning in his gaze. "Meera! What's wrong? Are you—?"

She collapsed against the counter, her face draining of color, eyes fluttering as if fighting an unseen force. Her breaths came in shallow gasps, each one more ragged than the last. Her body trembled, her hands clutching her chest as if trying to hold herself together. He reached out, trembling, clutching her shoulders as if anchoring her to life itself. Tears welled in his eyes, helpless and desperate.

"Arjun... I... I don't feel right," she whispered, voice trembling, tears spilling down her cheeks. "Something's wrong... I can't breathe..." Her face contorted in pain, eyes wide with fear. She looked at him—her anchor, her love—and in that moment, her expression shattered into pure agony. "Please... don't let me go," she begged, voice trembling with a mixture of fear and love.

He held her tighter, voice breaking. "No, no, no! Stay with me, Meera! Please, stay with me—don't leave me, don't leave me—"

The ambulance arrived just as her eyes fluttered closed, her body going limp. The rush of sirens filled the air like a cruel echo of hope. The doctors fought desperately, but it was too late. Her heart had stopped—silent, final, as if it had decided its time had come, leaving Arjun cradling an empty shell of the woman he loved.

He fell to his knees, tears streaming down his face, voice choked with grief. "Why? Why now? After everything... after all we've been through... How could this happen?"

The storm outside raged on, relentless and unyielding, mirroring the chaos inside his shattered soul.

Scene 9: The Weight of Silence

The silence she left behind was not merely quiet—it was an unbearable, crushing void that echoed through every corner of the house, deafening in its emptiness. It haunted him like a relentless ghost, whispering her absence into every breath he took. The kitchen counter where she'd stood that morning felt frozen in time, the faint, lingering scent of her perfume like a cruel ghost mocking his pain. Her brush sat untouched on the easel, the unfinished painting—a silent, cruel reminder of her absence, like a sentence left hanging and broken.

Arjun drifted through the days like a lost soul, hollow and broken. He stopped shaving, his reflection in the mirror unrecognizable—disheveled, gaunt, a shell of the man he once was. The garden she tended with such love had withered into a sickly, colorless wasteland, mirroring the darkness inside him. Calls from friends went unanswered, their voices fading into the void. The manuscript he had poured himself into—once a symbol of hope—gathered dust in a forgotten corner of his study, its pages yellowed and neglected, just like his fading dreams.

The ache of missing her was a constant, unbearable ache—an emptiness that hollowed out his chest. No matter how much time passed, her absence clawed at him, a relentless ache that refused to fade. He longed to hear her voice again, to see her smile, to feel her warm hand in his once more. Every night, he closed his eyes and imagined her there, whispering softly, her warmth a cruel memory he couldn't reach. The silence was deafening, and the ache of missing her threatened to drown him in a grief so deep it felt endless, unbreakable, consuming every fragment of his broken heart.

He often caught himself reaching out in the darkness, desperate to hold onto her, only to find emptiness. His mind replayed their last moments together, each memory a stabbing reminder of what was lost forever. The pain of missing her was a wound that refused to heal, an echo that haunted his every waking moment and every restless sleep. The void she left behind was a chasm he was terrified he would never cross, a grief so raw it threatened to swallow him whole—an ache that would never fade.

Scene 10: Resilience Through Memory

One evening, as the sun dipped below the horizon, casting a warm, amber glow across the sky, Arjun found himself in Meera's studio—a sacred space filled with her dreams, her passions, her unfinished work. The room was silent except for the faint whisper of the breeze through the window. On the easel stood her latest painting—a swirling explosion of blues and golds, vibrant and alive, yet hauntingly incomplete. It was as if her spirit still lingered there, caught in the midst of creation, waiting to be finished.

He stepped closer, his legs heavy with grief, and reached out with trembling fingers. His hand hovered above the canvas, hesitant, as if afraid to disturb the fragile beauty she had left behind. His fingertips brushed the rough surface, trembling with longing and hope. His voice cracked as he whispered, "You never left anything unfinished, Meera." Tears welled in his eyes, trembling as they spilled down his cheeks. "Why this? Why leave it like this?"

A surge of emotion overwhelmed him—an aching, desperate hope that somehow, she was still watching, still alive in some way. That maybe, just maybe, her spirit lingered here, waiting to return, waiting to finish what she started. His heart clenched with longing, yearning for her to walk through the door, to speak, to reassure him that she was still with him in some form.

The weight of loss pressed down on him, suffocating, until a fragile memory flickered to life—something she had said not long before her passing. Her voice, soft yet resolute, echoed in his mind: "Retirement isn't about stopping, Arjun. It's about creating something new—something meaningful. Build a life that honors what we've built together."

Her words, steady and unwavering, pierced through the fog of his despair. They rooted him in a fragile hope—that her spirit, her essence, was still somewhere nearby, watching, waiting for him to find the strength to carry on. The studio, once filled with silence and sorrow, now felt infused with a renewed purpose—a whisper of her strength guiding him, a silent promise that she might return, that their love was not truly gone but simply waiting to be reborn.

Scene 11: Finding Purpose

The next morning, Arjun stepped softly into the overgrown garden, where wild vines clung to the broken trellises and flowers drooped in silent surrender. Nature had claimed its space, the blooms faded and drooping, yet beneath the chaos, the promise of life still whispered in the soil—an unspoken vow that renewal was possible. He knelt down, fingers trembling as they sank into the earth, feeling its cool, forgiving embrace. In that quiet connection, a strange sense of closeness blossomed—an unspoken understanding that even in decay, there was hope.

"This was your sanctuary, Meera," he murmured, voice trembling with reverence and longing. "Maybe it can help me, too."

With tentative hands, he began to tend to the chaos—pulling weeds, watering the wilted petals, whispering words of love and forgiveness to the trembling earth. Each small act—each carefully rooted flower, each tender touch—felt like a fragile act of healing, a gentle awakening of the broken parts within him. It was not just the soil he was nurturing, but the pieces of himself buried beneath grief, regret, and love. Slowly, painfully, he learned that in tending to the garden, he was tending to his own wounded heart, one fragile bloom at a time.

Later, driven by a silent hope, he returned to her studio—her sacred space of dreams and colors. His trembling hands grasped her brush, feeling the weight of her absence and the faint echo of her touch. With a breath caught in his throat, he picked up where she had left off, finishing the painting she had begun. It was imperfect—flawed, raw, unfinished—yet in every stroke, he sensed her spirit stirring, breathing life into the colors once more. It wasn't just a painting; it was a fragment of her soul, resurrected from the depths of longing and love. And in that imperfect masterpiece, he found a strange, quiet solace—that somehow, someway, she was still there, alive in the vibrant whisper of the colors, in the breath of the brush, in the hope of new beginnings.

Scene 12: The First Page

On the first anniversary of Meera's passing, Arjun sat on the weathered porch, trembling slightly as he cradled a steaming cup of masala chai. The garden around him was in full bloom again—vivid, bursting with life—just as she had left it. Yet, beneath the beauty, his heart ached with an unbearable void, a hollow ache that refused to fade. Every flower, every leaf, was a silent testament to her absence, yet somehow, also a reminder of her love that still lingered—alive in the very soil she had nurtured.

He clutched the manuscript tightly in his trembling hands. The title, *The Last Chapter, the First Page,* was scrawled across the top in hurried, shaky handwriting—an act of defiance against the grief that threatened to drown him. His voice was barely more than a whisper, thick with emotion, as he spoke to the empty air:

"I thought losing you was the end," he whispered, each word trembling with the weight of a thousand shattered hopes. "But maybe... maybe it's just the last chapter of one book and the first page of another."

His eyes, red-rimmed and swollen from tears, stared into the fading sunlight, which cast a golden glow over the garden, illuminating the vibrant blossoms that stood resilient, defying the darkness. In that moment, Arjun felt something new—an ache that was not despair but a quiet, stubborn resilience. It was as if her love had become part of the very fabric of his being—woven into the roots of the garden, embedded in the strokes of her unfinished paintings, etched into the pages of his manuscript, and echoing in his heart.

He remembered her lessons—her words about planning, about creating joy even amid sorrow, about building a life filled with meaning and love. Her voice, soft yet firm, had once told him: *"Even in loss, there is a seed of hope. You just have to nurture it."*

And now, standing there, feeling the cool breeze on his face, Arjun realized—this wasn't the end. No, it was a new beginning. A chapter he hadn't expected, but one that shimmered with the promise of something different—something beautiful. Her love wasn't gone; it had transformed, become the quiet strength that carried him forward. It was in the garden's blooms, in the colors of her paintings, in the pages of his story.

This was not closure. It was hope—hope that even in the absence, love persisted. That her spirit was still with him, guiding him, whispering that something new, something extraordinary, was waiting just beyond the horizon. And in that fragile, trembling hope, Arjun found a flicker of peace—one that promised that love, no matter how lost, would always find a way to bloom again.

Something beautiful.

Scene 13: The Arrival of Krishna – Awakening the Warrior Within

In the quiet aftermath of days heavy with grief and self-doubt, Arjun sat in his study, the pages of his journal untouched, the pen idle in his hand. Shadows of a life once structured drifted across the room, echoing the hollowness he felt within.

It was then that the door creaked open.

Krishna.

Dressed simply, carrying an unspoken serenity, Krishna's presence filled the room with a stillness that stilled the noise in Arjun's heart. An old friend, yes—but more than that, he had always been a mirror to Arjun's soul, a voice of clarity in chaos.

"Arjun," Krishna said, his smile quiet and knowing, "you carry the weight of a battlefield in your eyes."

Arjun didn't deny it. "I feel like I've lost my way, Krishna.

Retirement has emptied my days. Rishi has moved on. Meera's illness has carved a hollow into my chest. I don't know who I am anymore."

Krishna stepped closer, not with pity, but with the strength of someone who had seen despair and led others through it.

"Then perhaps it is time," he said gently, "for you to remember who you are—not as a doctor, a husband, or a father—but as a soul, eternal and undiminished.

The Arjun who once stood tall in the face of fear still lives within you."

Arjun's gaze lifted slowly. There was something in Krishna's presence—a stillness deeper than peace—that invited strength without force.

Krishna placed a hand on his shoulder. "Walk with me. Let me remind you what the Gita once taught you—not just words, but truths for this very moment."

Scene 14: Lessons from the Bhagavad Gita – The Rebirth of a Warrior

As they sat beneath the neem tree in the courtyard, the twilight painting long shadows across the earth, Krishna began—not with sermons, but with simple truths that spoke straight to Arjun's fractured spirit.

"1. The Path of Duty Without Attachment (Karma Yoga)
You have a right to perform your duties, but never to the fruits of your actions."

Krishna looked into Arjun's eyes.
"You poured yourself into medicine, into family, with love. Now pour the same into your writing, your teaching, your being. Do not wait for applause. Act, because action is divine. Create without craving. Serve without expectation."

Arjun nodded, feeling the first stirrings of purpose that came not from the world's approval, but from within.

"2. Embracing Change as Divine (Impermanence)
As a person puts on new garments, giving up old ones, the soul similarly accepts new bodies..."

"Why mourn a chapter closing, Arjun?" Krishna asked softly. "You have not died. You are transforming. Meera is changing. Rishi is growing. Change is not loss—it is motion. You are not being left behind—you are being invited to evolve."

A tear slid down Arjun's cheek, not of sorrow, but of release.

"3. Equanimity in All Things (Samatvam)
Perform your duty with balance in success and failure. That balance is yoga."

"You have faced both triumph and despair, Arjun," Krishna continued. "But who are you beneath both? Resilience is not hardness. It is flexibility. Be like the bamboo—firm in root, soft in sway."

Arjun took a deep breath, as if inhaling strength from the very air.

"4. *Trust in the Unseen Path (Faith)*

Whatever happened, happened for good.
Whatever is happening, is for good.
Whatever will happen, will also be for good."

Krishna's voice was like a lamp in a dark corridor.

"There is a current beneath your life, Arjun. Even now, when Meera falters, when silence stretches across your halls—there is grace. Not all battles are fought on fields. Some are fought in silence, in surrender, in stillness."

As the stars began to blink awake in the sky, Arjun felt something shift. Not an answer, but a remembrance. The warrior within him—once fierce in the operating room, once unshaken in family crises—had not left. He had only paused, waiting for Arjun to look inward.

Krishna rose. "You are not broken, Arjun. You are awakening."

And with that, he walked into the night, leaving behind not silence, but the echo of resilience—spiritual, enduring, and deeply human.

The First Page

Epilogue

"The Last Chapter, The First Page"

Scene: Book Launch Evening – A Literary Festival Stage

The hall is softly lit. Warm pools of light fall on the stage. A modest lectern stands center, adorned with a vase of white lilies and a single copy of the newly launched book. Murmurs quiet as the emcee announces the final speaker.

"Ladies and gentlemen, please welcome the author of *The Last Chapter, the First Page*—Dr. Arjun Malhotra."

Applause rises. Arjun steps onto the stage with calm confidence, dressed in a simple kurta and shawl. He rests a hand briefly on the book before looking up at the audience, his voice steady and resonant.

ARJUN (speaking):

Good evening.

If someone had told me two years ago that I'd be standing here, launching a book, I would've smiled... and quietly changed the subject.

Not out of disbelief, but because I genuinely thought my story had already been told.

I retired from a life filled with meaning—surgery, teaching, healing—and stepped into silence.

> *"Not peaceful silence, but the kind that echoes.*
> *The kind that asks difficult questions at midnight."*

And then I lost Meera.

He pauses, eyes distant but composed. A breath.

She wasn't just my wife. She was the rhythm of my days. The grounding force. And when she was gone, I didn't know who I was anymore.

> *"The house grew quieter.*
> *The days longer.*
> *Grief is strange—it doesn't knock.*

It simply moves in, rearranges the furniture of your soul."

But as always, grace comes quietly.

One morning, my old friend Krishna visited—calm as ever, eyes full of that ageless wisdom. He reminded me of the Gita. Of the strength that lies not in resistance, but surrender with faith.

"*Krishna said, "Resilience is not about avoiding the storm.*
It's about walking through it, with open arms."

And then came Sanya.

He looks toward a figure in the front row—offstage. A soft smile.

A mentor, not by profession, but by presence. She saw the fragments I carried and helped me see the mosaic they could become.

"*She once told me, "Grief isn't the end of the book.*
It's the turning of a page. But only you can write what comes next."

So I began.

A sentence. A sketch. A memory.

What emerged was not just a manuscript, but a resurrection.

He holds the book gently in both hands.

This is a tribute.

To Meera's unshakeable grace.

To the stillness that follows storms.

To the resilience that doesn't roar—but endures, quietly.

It's not about loss.

It's about love.

It's about the courage to begin again.

He closes the book, sets it down carefully.

"*To those of you facing the great unknown—retirement, grief,*
change—this is my message:
You are not at the end.
You are standing at a new beginning.
Pick up the pen.
Write the next chapter.
Let your life become the story it was always meant to be."

Thank you.

Silence hangs for a heartbeat. Then, the audience rises in applause. Arjun bows gently.

"*As the lights dim, he walks offstage—not as someone who has finished something,*

but as someone who has finally begun."

Dr. Arjun Malhotra had not just survived retirement. He had transcended it.

Arjun's journey exemplifies the themes of resilience, personal growth, and the power of love and communication in relationships.

His story serves as a poignant reminder that while loss is inevitable, the connections we nurture and the passions we pursue can lead to a fulfilling life,

even during challenging transitions.

The relationships we cultivate and the legacies we honor can provide the strength to navigate the complexities of life.

CHAPTER 2 : Understanding Priorities

I. The General Aspects

A. Understanding Burnout:

Burnout, characterized by emotional, physical, and mental exhaustion, is increasingly recognized in high-pressure work environment.

Symptoms can include chronic fatigue, irritability, and a sense of disconnection from work. Recognizing these signs early allows you to take proactive steps to address them.

By identifying the sources of burnout, such as

- High workload and job demands leading to stress and exhaustion.
- Lack of work-life balance, making it difficult to fulfill family responsibilities.
- Limited support and resources from the organization.
- Unrealistic expectations and pressure to constantly perform at a high level.
- Poor management practices, including lack of communication and feedback.

we can focus on creating a more manageable workload through effective time management and delegation.

a. The Importance of Resilience

Resilience is the ability to adapt and recover from adversity, a critical skill for senior professionals .

It empowers individuals to navigate challenges effectively, maintain focus, and make sound decisions under pressure.

The components of resilience, includes emotional regulation, problem-solving skills, and the value of a strong support network, often found within extended family and community. leveraging family's support during challenging times, turning obstacles into opportunities for growth and learning is a good way.

b. Self-Assessment and Reflection

Self-assessment is a critical step in building resilience.

Keeping a reflective journal can help you evaluate your feelings, thoughts, and behaviors, allowing for a deeper understanding of your stressors and emotional responses.

EXERCISE

Identify Sources of Burnout

- What specific aspects of your work contribute to stress?

- How do you feel emotionally on a daily basis?

B. Establishing Boundaries

Setting clear boundaries is essential for maintaining a healthy work-life balance, especially in Indian culture where family commitments often overlap with professional responsibilities. Defining your work hours and communicating them to colleagues helps protect your time and energy, leading to improved well-being and productivity.

a. Prioritizing Self-Care
Self-care is crucial for resilience. This can be explored through various aspects of physical and mental health, including traditional practices like yoga and Ayurveda, alongside modern exercise, nutrition, and mindfulness practices.

b. Professional Development
Investing in your professional growth is vital for maintaining job satisfaction. It encourages you to seek out continuous learning opportunities, such as workshops, conferences, and mentorship programs available.

c. Building Social Support
In Indian culture, family and community play a pivotal role in providing emotional support. Cultivating relationships with colleagues, friends, and family can provide emotional sustenance during challenging times.

d. Achieving Work-Life Balance
Finding balance between work and personal life is essential for mental well-being. Engage in hobbies that resonate with Indian culture, such as music, dance, or cooking, and set aside time for relaxation during festivals or family gatherings.

II. The Key aspects:

A. Cultivating a Positive Mindset:

A positive mindset is a cornerstone of resilience. It shapes how you perceive challenges and influences your emotional well-being. Cultivating positivity involves adopting an optimistic outlook, practicing gratitude, and recognizing the potential for growth in every experience.

a. **Positive Thinking:**
Positive thinking is not about ignoring difficulties but rather approaching them with a constructive attitude. It encourages you to focus on solutions rather than problems. Research has shown that maintaining a positive outlook can lead to better stress management and improved overall health.

b. **Practice Gratitude:**
Gratitude has profound effects on mental health. Taking time to acknowledge what you are thankful for can shift your focus from stressors to the positive aspects of your life. This practice doesn't require elaborate rituals; it can be as simple as reflecting on three things you appreciate each day.

c. **Affirmation:**

Incorporating positive affirmations into your daily routine can further reinforce a positive mindset. These are simple, positive statements that you repeat to yourself to challenge negative thoughts and boost confidence.

"Dr. Verma began a daily gratitude practice, jotting down her thoughts in a journal. Over time, she noticed a shift in her mindset, leading to increased resilience in the face of professional challenges".

Exercise:

Keep a Gratitude Journal

Write three things you are grateful for each day:

1. ____

2. ____

3. ____

Positive Affirmations

Write three affirmations that resonate with you:

1. ____

2. ____

3. ____

B. Emergency Strategies:

Life can be unpredictable, and having strategies in place to manage overwhelming moments is crucial for maintaining resilience. This chapter focuses on developing a personal crisis plan and identifying quick coping mechanisms that can help you regain control during stressful situations.

a. Identifying Triggers:
Understanding what triggers your stress is the first step in developing effective coping strategies. Common triggers might include unexpected work demands, family issues, or personal health challenges. By identifying these triggers, you can prepare yourself to handle them more effectively.

b. Coping Mechanisms :
Develop a list of coping strategies that work for you.
These could include:
1. Deep Breathing: A simple technique to calm your mind and reduce stress.
2. Mindfulness Meditation: Taking a few minutes to focus on your breath can help ground you.
3. Physical Activity: Engaging in physical exercise can serve as a powerful stress reliever
c. Support Network:
Don't hesitate to reach out to friends, family, or colleagues for support during crises. Having a trusted person to talk to can provide additional perspective and help alleviate feelings of isolation

"During a particularly stressful period, Dr. Rao implemented a crisis plan that included taking a short walk during breaks and practicing deep breathing exercises. These strategies helped him regain composure and focus during challenging moments."

Exercise:

Create a Crisis Plan
Write down three quick strategies you can use when feeling overwhelmed:

1. ____

2. ____

3. ____

C. Implementation and Follow-Up

Setting specific goals and monitoring your progress is crucial for building resilience and ensuring that your retirement planning stays on track.

This chapter will guide you through the process of implementing the strategies discussed in this e-handbook and encourage regular follow-up to assess your growth.

a. Setting SMART Goals:
When establishing your goals, consider using the SMART criteria:

- Specific: Clearly define what you want to achieve
- Measurable: Establish criteria for measuring progress
- Achievable: Set realistic goals that are attainable
- Relevant: Ensure your goals align with your overall objectives.
- Time-bound: Set a deadline for achieving your goals.

b. Regular Check-Ins:
Schedule regular check-ins with yourself to review your progress. This can be weekly or monthly, depending on what works best for you. Use these check-ins to reflect on your achievements, reassess your goals, and make adjustments as necessary.

c. Accountability:
Consider sharing your goals with a trusted friend or mentor who can help keep you accountable. Having someone to discuss your journey with can provide motivation and encouragement.

"Dr. Singh set a goal to participate in a leadership workshop within three months. During his monthly check-ins, he assessed his progress and adjusted his schedule to prioritize learning opportunities, ultimately enhancing his professional skills".

Exercise:

Set Specific Goals - Identify two immediate actions to implement this plan:
    1. Action: ____
               by _______________.

    2. Action: _______________________________________
              by _____________

III. The Vital Aspects

1. Building Financial Resilience

In addition to emotional and physical well-being, financial health plays a crucial role in the resilience of senior professionals.

Stress related to finances can significantly impact your mental health, productivity, and overall quality of life.

Understanding how to manage your money effectively is an essential skill that contributes to your ability to navigate life's challenges with confidence and stability.

The Connection Between Financial Health and Resilience

Financial stress can heighten anxiety and overwhelm, reducing your ability to focus on work and personal aspirations.

For senior professionals, effective money management can offer peace of mind, allowing greater energy and commitment to both career and personal growth.

On the other hand, poor financial choices often increase stress, affecting both performance and health.

"Dr. Aruna, a seasoned academic, encountered unexpected medical expenses. The financial strain distracted her from her research and teaching, causing feelings of inadequacy and burnout. Realizing the importance of financial control, she adopted practical money management strategies, gradually reclaiming her confidence and stability.

A. Key Strategies for Effective Money Management

a. Create a Budget:

A budget is a cornerstone of financial planning.

It helps you track income, categorize expenses, and set savings goals.

Start by documenting all income sources and dividing expenses into fixed (e.g., rent, bills) and variable (e.g., leisure, dining out).

Income: ____

Fixed Expenses: _______________________________________

Variable Expenses: ____________________________________

Savings Goals: ____

b. Emergency Fund:

An emergency fund acts as a buffer for unexpected costs, protecting you from financial setbacks.

Aim to save enough to cover three to six months of essential expenses.

Current Savings: ______________________________________

Target Savings: _______________________________________

Steps to Reach Target: ________________________________

c. Debt /Loan Management:

Addressing debt is key to financial resilience.
Prioritize paying off high-interest obligations like credit cards.
Methods such as the snowball or avalanche techniques can help.

d. Investing for the Future:

Investing helps build long-term wealth.
Categorise your investment for short, mid and long terms.
Choose options that align with your risk tolerance and retirement plans—such as EPG,PPF, stocks, or mutual funds.

e. Seek Professional Advice:

If financial management seems daunting, a certified advisor can help clarify options and
build a personalized plan based on your goals and needs.

B. Cultivating a Positive Money Mindset

Maintaining a healthy attitude toward money is crucial. Many experience guilt or anxiety around finances, but remember that managing money is a learned skill. Be kind to yourself and celebrate milestones, no matter how small.

Positive Affirmations for Financial Health:-

- **I am capable of managing my finances effectively.**
- **I make informed financial decisions that align with my goals.**
- **I am building a secure and stable financial future.**

C. The Importance of Regular Review

Financial management should be revisited regularly. Set aside monthly time to revise your budget, check on your savings and investment goals, and make adjustments as needed. This habit keeps your financial decisions informed and proactive.

In summary, mastering financial management strengthens your resilience as a senior professional. By proactively managing your finances, you reduce stress and empower yourself to thrive in both personal and professional realms. With consistency and patience, financial resilience is within your reach

2. The Role of Spirituality in Resilience

Spirituality can be a profound source of strength and resilience, particularly in times of personal or professional upheaval. For many individuals, it offers a framework for understanding life's challenges, a sense of purpose, and a community of support. In the context of retirement and the transitions that come with it, spirituality can play a pivotal role in helping individuals navigate their emotions and experiences.

A.Finding Meaning in Transitions

One of the primary ways spirituality enhances resilience is by providing a sense of meaning and purpose. During significant life changes, such as retirement or an empty nest, individuals may grapple with questions of identity and relevance. Spiritual practices—whether they involve prayer, meditation, or contemplation—can help individuals reconnect with their core values and beliefs. This introspection allows them to frame their experiences not as endings but as new beginnings filled with potential.

Reflective Journaling:

Write about what retirement means to you. What are your hopes and fears?

Reflect on the skills and passions you want to explore in this new chapter.

Frequency: Set aside 10-15 minutes each week to write.

B. Cultivating Inner Peace:

Spirituality often encourages practices that cultivate inner peace and mindfulness, such as meditation, yoga, or reflective journaling. These practices can help individuals manage stress and anxiety, which are common during transitions. By fostering a sense of calm, spirituality allows individuals to approach challenges with clarity and composure.

Mindfulness Meditation:

Instructions: Find a quiet space. Sit comfortably and close your eyes. Focus on your breath, inhaling deeply through your nose and exhaling through your mouth. If your mind wanders, gently bring your focus back to your breath.

Duration: Start with 5 minutes daily, gradually increasing to 10-15 minutes.

3. Building Community and Support

Spirituality often fosters a sense of community, providing individuals with a network of support during challenging times. Whether through religious congregations, spiritual groups, or mindfulness communities, these connections can offer emotional sustenance, encouragement, and a shared sense of purpose.

Join a Community Group:

Action: Research local spiritual or meditation groups. Attend a session to connect with others who share similar values and experiences.

Goal: Aim to participate in at least one group activity per month.

a. Resilience Through Faith and Hope

For many, spirituality is deeply intertwined with faith and hope. Believing in a higher power or a greater purpose can instill a sense of hope during difficult times. This hope acts as a buffer against despair, reminding individuals that challenges are often temporary and that there is a broader context to their experiences.

Daily Affirmations:

Instructions: Create a list of positive affirmations related to your spiritual beliefs and resilience.

For example: "I am guided by a higher purpose," or "I embrace change with grace."

Practice: Repeat these affirmations each morning to set a positive tone for your day.

b. Embracing Change and Letting Go

Spirituality also encourages the acceptance of change and the practice of letting go. Many spiritual traditions emphasize the impermanence of life and the importance of adapting to new circumstances. This mindset can foster resilience by helping individuals view transitions not as losses but as opportunities for renewal.

Letting Go Ceremony:

Instructions: Write down things you feel you need to let go of—fears, regrets, or attachments. Find a meaningful way to release these—perhaps by burning the paper in a safe space or burying it in the ground.

Reflection:

After the ceremony, take a moment to reflect on how releasing these burdens can open up space for new opportunities

Conclusion

In summary, spirituality plays a vital role in building resilience, particularly during significant life transitions. By providing meaning, cultivating inner peace, fostering community, and instilling hope, spirituality empowers individuals to navigate challenges with grace and strength. As Meera and Arjun embark on their journey into retirement, their spiritual beliefs can serve as a guiding light, helping them embrace change and discover new pathways for personal growth and fulfillment. Incorporating these simple exercises into daily life can enhance their spiritual journey, reinforcing their resilience and capacity to thrive in this new chapter.

3. Retirement Planning

Retirement planning is a crucial aspect of financial management that significantly impacts your quality of life in your later years. For senior professionals, particularly those in demanding fields such as medicine and academia, the transition to retirement can bring a mix of excitement and anxiety.

A well-thought-out retirement plan not only ensures financial security but also provides a roadmap for maintaining a fulfilling lifestyle after your professional life.

The Importance of Retirement Planning:
Many individuals underestimate the importance of retirement planning, often believing that they can simply rely on Social Security or employer-sponsored retirement plans. However, these sources may not provide sufficient income to maintain your desired lifestyle. According to financial experts, it is advisable to aim for a retirement income that is about 70-80% of your pre-retirement income.

"Dr. Tiwari, a senior orthopaedic professor, learned this lesson the hard way when he faced unexpected medical expenses shortly after retiring. Although he had saved diligently, he hadn't accounted for the rising costs of healthcare. This experience underscored the importance of comprehensive retirement planning."

A. Key Components of a Retirement Plan:

a. Assess Your Retirement Needs:

Begin by determining your retirement goals. Consider factors such as desired lifestyle, travel plans, hobbies, and potential healthcare needs. Estimate your expected expenses in retirement, including housing, food, healthcare, and leisure activities.

Estimate Your Retirement Expenses

Monthly Living Expenses: _______________________________

Healthcare Costs: ____________________________________

Travel and Leisure: __________________________________

Other Expenses: _____________________________________

(More Details can be done in Chapter 3 workbook section)

b. Calculate Your Retirement Income:

Identify potential sources of income during retirement. This may include:
Social Security benefits
Employer-sponsored retirement plans
Personal savings and investments
Rental income or part-time work

List Your Retirement Income Sources

Source: _________________ Amount: _____________

Source: _________________ Amount: _____________

(More Details can be done in Chapter 3 workbook section)

c. Create a Savings Strategy:

If you are still in your working years, it's crucial to develop a robust savings strategy. Aim to maximize contributions to retirement accounts, taking advantage of employer matches when available.

Develop Your Savings Plan in terms of :

Current Savings Rate: _______________________________________

Target Savings Rate: _______________________________________

Adjustments Needed: _______________________________________

(More Details can be done in Chapter 3 workbook section)

d. Invest Wisely:

Your investment strategy will play a significant role in your retirement savings. Consider your risk tolerance, investment horizon, and the need for growth versus capital preservation. Diversifying your portfolio across different asset classes can help mitigate risk.

Review Your Investment Strategy

Current Investment Allocation: _______________________________

Desired Allocation: _______________________________________

Adjustments Needed: _______________________________________

(More Details can be done in Chapter 3 workbook section)

e. Plan for Healthcare Costs:

Healthcare expenses can be one of the most significant financial burdens in retirement. Research options for Medicare, supplemental insurance, and long-term care insurance.

Factor these costs into your retirement budget.

Assess Your Healthcare Needs

Anticipated Healthcare Costs: _______________________________

Insurance Coverage: _______________________________

((More Details can be done in Chapter 3 workbook section)

f. Consider Legacy Planning:

Many professionals wish to leave a legacy for their families or communities.

Consider how you want to allocate your assets after your passing, and consult with a financial advisor or estate planner to create a will or trust.

Outline Your Legacy Goals

a. Beneficiaries: _______________________________

b. Charitable Contributions: _______________________________

(More Details can be done in Chapter 3 workbook section)

B. Cultivating a Positive Mindset About Retirement:

Retirement can evoke a range of emotions, from anticipation to fear. Cultivating a positive mindset about this transition is important. Embrace the idea that retirement is an opportunity for new beginnings, exploration, and personal growth. Engage in hobbies or activities you've always wanted to pursue but didn't have time for during your career.

Positive Affirmations for Retirement Planning

- I am prepared for a fulfilling retirement.
- I embrace new opportunities and adventures in my next chapter.
- I have the financial resources to enjoy my retirement.

C. The Importance of Regular Review:

Retirement planning is not a one-time event; it requires regular review and adjustment. As your financial situation, goals, and market conditions change, it's essential to revisit your retirement plan to ensure it remains aligned with your objectives.

Set aside time annually to assess your retirement savings, investment performance, and overall financial health. This practice will help you stay on track and make informed decisions regarding your future

In conclusion, effective retirement planning is an essential component of financial management for senior professionals. By taking the time to assess your needs, calculate your income, and create a savings strategy, you can ensure a secure and fulfilling retirement. Remember that this process is ongoing, and regular review will help you stay aligned with your goals as you transition into this new phase of life.

3

CHAPTER 3: Workbook Section

This workbook section provides a structured approach to tracking progress and implementing the strategies outlined in the e-handbook. It encourages active engagement and reflection, making it a practical tool for senior professionals as they work toward building resilience and planning for a fulfilling retirement.

A. Building Resilience - A dozen ways

1. Develop a Strong Support System

List 5 people you can turn to for support.

1.
2.
3
4
5

"Schedule a catch-up with one person this week."

Reflection

2. Practice Self-Care
Create a weekly self-care plan
Exercise
Diet
Sleep

"Include at least one mindfulness practice"

3. Cultivate a Positive Mindset

Write down three negative thoughts you often have.

1

2

3

4. Reframe each into a positive thought

1

2

3

5. Set Realistic Goals

Identify a goal you want to achieve. Break it down into 3 smaller, achievable steps

1

2

3

6. Enhance Problem-Solving Skills

Choose a recent problem . List possible solutions. Reflect on what you learned from the experience

7. Embrace Change

Write down a recent change you've faced.Identify how you adapted and what you learned

52

8. Build Emotional Awareness

Keep a daily journal of your emotions for a week. Reflect on patterns or triggers you notice.

Sun

Mon

Tues

Wed

Thurs

Fri

Sat

9. Foster a Sense of Purpose

List your top 3 values. Write one action you can take this week that aligns with those values

1

2

3

10. Limit Exposure to Stressors

Identify your main stressors (news, social media, etc.).

Set boundaries (e.g., limit time or specific times to engage).

11. Practice Resilience-Building Activities

List 3 hobbies or activities that recharge you.

"Schedule time for at least one this week."

12. What challenges have you faced recently?

How did you respond, and what did you learn about your resilience?

57

What strategies from this workbook do you feel will be most beneficial for you?

Action Plan

Goal

Steps to Achieve

Timeline

Support Needed

Monthly Progress Tracking Table

A. What **insights have you gained about yourself and your resilience**?

Exercise :

a. Identify Sources of Burnout.

b. List specific stressors.

c. Define **Your Work Hour**s Work hours: _______ to _______.

d. **Create a Self-Care Plan**

Physical activities:

e. Identify **Development Opportunities**

Workshops or courses to attend:

B. Money Management

Exercise:

Create a Budget.

List the Sources of income Amount

List the Expenses. Amount

Assess Your **Emergency Fund**

Current savings
Target savings

List Your **Debts/ Loans**

Debts/ Loans. Amounts Interest rates.

Evaluate **Your Investment Strategy**

Current Investments

Retirement Investments

Identify **Potential Advisors**

List names and contact information for financial advisors.

1.

2.

C. Retirement Planning

Exercise:

Estimate Your Retirement Expenses

Monthly expenses
Living
Health Care
Food
Travel
Other

List Your Retirement Income Sources
Identify sources of income during retirement.

64

Develop Your Savings Plan

Current savings rate:

Target savings rate:

Review Your Investment Strategy

Current Investments:

Desired investment allocation:

Bank (Term Deposits)

Market

Gold etc

Real Estate

others

Assess Your Healthcare Needs

A. Routine Half yeallry Checkups : Schedule date/ Hospital name / Doctor name / Support identifed.

B. List Illness /Probable Sequelae / Doctor name for Primary care / Hospital name for Advance care

C. Insurance which cover aboe and routine checkups

Outline Your Legacy Goals-Will

Beneficiaries / Details of istribution/ Name of Lawyer or Guardian
Charitable contributions / Details / Guardian for distribution.
Place and person to contact after Death for Will :

D. Track Your Journey to Resilience and Retirement

This is a practical tool to help you document your reflections, set goals, and monitor your progress as you work towards building resilience and planning for a fulfilling retirement.

Use the exercises in this section to reinforce the concepts discussed in the book.

1. Identifying Sources of Burnout

Reflect on the specific stressors in your professional and personal life.

Stressors

Impact on Well-Being

Action Steps to Address

2. Defining Your Work Hours

Establish clear boundaries for your work hours to maintain a healthy work-life balance.

Days of the Week. Work Hours. Key Tasks

Monday

Tuesday

Wednesday

Thursday

Firday

Saturday

3. Creating a Self-Care Plan

Outline a self-care plan that includes physical activities and nutrition goals.

Self-Care Activities. Frequency

1. Walking
2. Yoga/Strecthing
3. Gym/ Club
4.Jogging
5.Others

Nutrition Goals

Identify Dietery Requirement
Routine
Special
Daily Calories
Cook Your meal

4. Identifying Development Opportunities

List potential workshops, courses, or training programs that can enhance your skills.

Explore online oppurtunities too.

Opportunities. Provider/Institution. Date

5. Connecting with Colleagues

Schedule meetings or informal catch-ups with colleagues to build your support network.

Colleagues. Date for Meeting. Notes

6. Listing Hobbies and Interests: Identify activities outside of work that bring you joy and fulfillment.

Hobbies/Interests. Frequency. Notes

7. Keeping a Gratitude Journal

Reflect on three things you are grateful for each day.
Keep on generating the list , you may use a small diary for the same.

8. Creating a Crisis Plan

Develop a personal crisis plan that includes quick strategies for managing overwhelming moments.

Anticipated Crisis. Strategies. How to Implement

9. Setting Specific Goals

Define immediate actions to implement the strategies discussed in this workbook.

Goals. Action Steps. Deadline

Conclusion

As you approach retirement, remember that building resilience and effective financial management are essential for thriving in your golden years. By integrating the strategies outlined in this book into your life, you can enhance your well-being, achieve financial security, and enjoy a fulfilling retirement. Embrace the journey ahead with confidence and optimism.

E. Resilience Through Spirituality During Retirement Transition

This is designed to guide you through reflections, exercises, and practices that will help you navigate this significant life change with grace and strength. As you embark on this journey, remember that spirituality can provide a sense of purpose, connection, and inner peace.

A. Understanding the Transition

Reflection

What emotions are you experiencing as you approach retirement?

Write down your thoughts on what this transition means to you.

Identify Your Feelings:

List the emotions you feel about retirement:

B. **Finding Meaning in Retirement**

Reflection

Consider how your values and beliefs shape your understanding of retirement.

What new opportunities do you see for personal growth?

Reflective Journaling

Write about what retirement means to you in the context of your spirituality.

What new passions or skills do you want to explore?

C. Cultivating Inner Peace

Mindfulness Practice

- Dedicate a quiet space for daily mindfulness meditation (Dhyana).

Daily Mindfulness Meditation

Duration: Start with 5 minutes daily, gradually increasing to 15 minutes.
Instructions:
1. Sit comfortably in a quiet space.
2. Close your eyes and focus on your breath.
3. If your mind wanders, gently return your focus to your breath.
Reflection
How did you feel after your meditation session?

D. Building Community and Support

Reflection

Who are the key people in your life that can support you during this transition?

Community Connections

Identify local spiritual or community groups you can join.

Group Name Contact Information Meeting Frequency

E. Resilience Through Faith and Hope

Reflection

How does your faith or spiritual practice provide you hope during this transition?

Daily Affirmations (Sankalp)

Create three affirmations that resonate with your spirituality.

Practice: Repeat these affirmations each morning.

F. Embracing Change and Letting Go
Reflection
What are the fears or attachments you need to let go of as you transition
into retirement?

Letting Go Ceremony (Tyaag)

Write down things you feel you need to release.

Choose a meaningful way to release these burdens, such as a small ritual or
a symbolic act like burning the paper or immersing it in water.

G Reflection and Action Plan

Reflection

After completing the exercises, what insights have you gained about your transition into retirement?

What steps will you take to ensure you remain resilient?

Create Your Action Plan

Identify actions you will take to nurture your spiritual resilience during retirement.

CHAPTER 4: To Do activities to keep Emotional and Physical Strength

A. 10 to do Activities to Strengthen Emotional Resilience During Life Transitions

1. Mindfulness and Meditation Practice

Tips

- Start with 5-minute guided meditations daily using apps like Calm or Headspace.
- Find a quiet space, sit comfortably, and focus on your breath.

Example:

Sit quietly each morning, breathe deeply, and gently acknowledge your thoughts without judgment. Gradually increase meditation time to 10-15 minutes.

2. Journaling and Self-Reflection

Tips:

- Keep a gratitude journal; write three things you are thankful for each day.
- Use prompts like "Today I felt..." or "I am grateful for..."

Example:

After a walk in the park, jot down feelings of peace or appreciation for nature's beauty.

3. Seeking Support through Counselling or Support Groups

Tips:
- Look for local or online support groups for grief or life changes.
- Don't hesitate to seek professional counselling if needed.

Example:

Join a grief support group where members share their journeys, helping you feel less alone.

4.*Engaging in Creative Arts (Painting, Music, Writing)*

Tips:
- Dedicate weekly time for a creative activity, regardless of skill level.
- Explore new hobbies like painting, playing an instrument, or writing.

Example:

Start a scrapbook of cherished memories or take a beginner's watercolor class

5. Connecting with Nature

Tips:
- Schedule outdoor activities regularly, like walking or gardening.
- Spend time observing and appreciating the natural world.

Example:

Plant flowers or vegetables, or take a slow walk in a nearby park.

6. Practicing Self-Compassion and Positive Affirmations

Tips:
- Write affirmations on sticky notes and place around your home.
- Repeat affirmations daily, especially during challenging moments.

Example:

Say, "I am enough," or "I deserve happiness," to nurture self-love.

7. Volunteering and Giving Back

Tips:

- Find local opportunities aligned with your interests, like mentoring or helping at community centers.
- Volunteering provides purpose and connection.
Example:
Volunteer at a soup kitchen or teach a hobby you love to others.

8. Building or Rebuilding Social Connections

Tips:
- Reach out to friends or family for calls or meetups.
- Join clubs or groups for seniors or shared interests.
Example:
Invite a neighbour for tea or join a local hobby group to foster friendships.

9. Engaging in Spiritual or Religious Practices

Tips:
- Attend community services, prayer groups, or spiritual gatherings.
- Practice meditation or prayer that resonates with your beliefs.
Example:
Participate in a meditation retreat or join a spiritual discussion group.

10. Physical Activity and Gentle Exercise

Tips:
- Incorporate 30-minute walks, yoga, or tai chi into your routine.
- Choose activities suitable for your fitness level.
Example:
Join a gentle yoga class or practice chair yoga at home to boost mood and flexibility.

Remember:

Building emotional strength is an ongoing process. Be patient with yourself, and embrace these activities as part of your self-care journey.

B. 10 Top to do for physical strengthening

1. Walking:

Tip:

Start with short walks and gradually increase the duration. Use proper walking shoes to support your feet.

Example:

Walk around your neighborhood, in a local park, or on a treadmill. Consider walking with a friend or joining a walking group for motivation.

2. Strength Training:

Tip:

Begin with light weights or resistance bands and focus on proper form. Increase weight gradually to avoid injury.

Example:

Perform exercises like squats, lunges, bicep curls, and shoulder presses. Consider using machines or free weights under supervision.

3. Yoga:

Tip:

Take classes specifically designed for seniors or beginners. Listen to your body and practice deep breathing for relaxation.

Example:

Try poses like Mountain Pose, Warrior I and II, Tree Pose, and Child's Pose. Use props like blocks and straps for support.

4. Swimming:

Tip:

Start with water walking or gentle swimming strokes. Use flotation devices if needed and swim in designated areas.

Example:

Swim laps in a pool, participate in water aerobics classes, or do water-based exercises for resistance training.

5. Cycling:

Tip:

Adjust the bike seat and handlebars to the correct height. Start with flat terrain before progressing to hills.

Example:

Ride a stationary bike at home or join a cycling group for outdoor rides. Consider using a recumbent bike for added comfort.

6. Tai Chi:

Tip:

Practice slow, controlled movements and focus on deep breathing. Attend classes led by a certified Tai Chi instructor.

Example:

Perform Tai Chi forms such as "Wave Hands Like Clouds," "Golden Rooster Stands on One Leg," and "Parting the Wild Horse's Mane."

7. Pilates:

Tip:

Engage your core muscles throughout each exercise. Start with beginner-level classes and progress as you build strength.

Example:

Try exercises like the Hundred, Leg Circles, the Swan, and the Side Leg Series. Use a Pilates reformer or mat for workouts.

8. Dancing:

Tip:

Choose dance styles that suit your fitness level and interests. Focus on footwork, coordination, and rhythm.

Example:

Dance to music at home, take ballroom dancing classes, enjoy line dancing, or try Zumba for a fun workout.

9. Water Aerobics:

Tip:

Wear water shoes for traction and join classes suitable for seniors. Pay attention to proper form and posture in the water.

Example:

Engage in water jogging, leg lifts, arm exercises, and water-based resistance training using foam dumbbells.

10. Stretching:

Tip:

Perform gentle stretches after a warm-up or at the end of your workout. Hold each stretch for 15-30 seconds and avoid bouncing.

Example:

Stretch major muscle groups such as hamstrings, quadriceps, calves, shoulders, and back. Use a stretching strap or towel for assistance.

"Incorporating a mix of these activities into your routine can help maintain physical strength, flexibility, and overall well-being in the later stages of life.
Remember to enjoy the process and listen to your body's needs while staying active."

C. 10 nutrition care tips for the last phase of life, to help maintain optimal health:

1. Stay Hydrated:

Tip:

Drink plenty of water throughout the day to prevent dehydration and promote overall health.

Example:

Carry a water bottle with you and set reminders to drink fluids regularly. Include hydrating foods like fruits, vegetables, and soups in your diet.

2. Focus on Nutrient-Dense Foods:

Tip:

Choose foods rich in nutrients like fruits, vegetables, whole grains, lean proteins, and healthy fats.

Example:

Include colorful salads, lean meats, whole grain pasta, nuts, seeds, and seafood in your meals to ensure a variety of nutrients.

3. Eat Adequate Protein:

Tip:

Consume protein-rich foods like lean meats, poultry, fish, eggs, dairy, legumes, and tofu to support muscle health and immune function.

Example:

Enjoy grilled chicken breast, salmon fillets, Greek yogurt, lentil soup, and scrambled eggs to meet your protein needs.

4. Include Calcium-Rich Foods:

Tip:

Maintain bone health by incorporating calcium-rich foods like dairy products, fortified plant-based milks, leafy greens, and tofu.

Example:

Have a glass of milk, yogurt with granola, kale salad, or a calcium-fortified smoothie as part of your daily intake.

5. Eat Fiber-Rich Foods:

Tip:

Support digestive health and regularity by including fiber-rich foods like whole grains, fruits, vegetables, nuts, seeds, and legumes.

Example:

Enjoy oatmeal with berries, quinoa salad, lentil soup, roasted vegetables, and chia seed pudding for fiber intake.

6. Limit Added Sugars and Sodium:

Tip:

Minimize intake of sugary beverages, desserts, processed foods, and high-sodium products to reduce the risk of chronic diseases.

Example:

Opt for fresh fruits for sweetness, read labels for hidden sugars, cook meals at home to control salt, and use herbs/spices for flavor.

7. Incorporate Healthy Fats:

Tip:

Include sources of healthy fats like avocados, nuts, seeds, olive oil, and fatty fish for heart health and brain function.

Example:

Drizzle olive oil on salads, snack on almonds, add avocado to sandwiches, and enjoy salmon for omega-3 fatty acids.

8. Eat Regularly and Mindfully

Tip:

Aim for regular, balanced meals and snacks to maintain energy levels. Eat slowly and savor your food for better digestion.

Example:

Plan meals with a combination of food groups, avoid skipping meals, sit down to eat without distractions, and listen to hunger/fullness cues.

9. Consider Nutritional Supplements:

Tip:

Consult a healthcare provider for guidance on appropriate supplements like vitamin D, B vitamins, calcium, or omega-3s based on individual needs.

Example:

Take supplements as recommended by your healthcare provider to fill nutrient gaps and support overall health.

10. Listen to Your Body:

Tip:

Pay attention to how certain foods make you feel and adjust your diet accordingly. Seek professional advice for specific dietary concerns.

Example:

Keep a food diary, note any digestive discomfort or changes in energy levels, and make informed choices based on your body's responses.

"By following these nutrition care tips and incorporating a variety of nutrient-rich foods into your diet, you can support your overall health and well-being during the later stages of life.
Remember to prioritize a balanced and enjoyable eating pattern that meets your individual nutritional needs and preferences."

D. To do 10 things to manage When facing chronic illnesses like diabetes, hypertension, cancer, renal failure, and heart disease.

1. Follow Medical Advice:

Tip:

Work closely with healthcare providers, ask questions, and adhere to treatment plans.

Example:

Attend regular check-ups, take medications as prescribed, and monitor blood sugar levels for diabetes.

2. Maintain a Healthy Diet:

Tip:

Focus on whole foods, limit processed items, and consult a dietitian for personalized meal plans.

Example:

Include meals like grilled and roasted vegetables to support heart health.

3. Regular Exercise:

Tip:

Choose activities you enjoy, start slowly, and aim for consistency in your workout routine.

Example:

Engage in activities like swimming, walking, or gentle yoga for physical and mental well-being.

4. Manage Stress:

Tip:

Practice relaxation techniques, prioritize self-care, and seek support from loved ones.

Example:

Schedule time for meditation, deep breathing exercises, or hobbies to reduce stress levels.

5. Get Sufficient Sleep:

Tip:

Create a bedtime routine, limit screen time before bed, and ensure a comfortable sleep environment.

Example:

Aim for 7-9 hours of sleep each night by going to bed and waking up at consistent times.

6. Monitor Vital Signs:

Tip:

Keep track of blood pressure, blood sugar, weight, and symptoms to manage your condition effectively.

Example:

Record daily blood pressure readings and food intake to identify patterns and share with your healthcare team.

7. Stay Informed:

Tip:

Educate yourself about your condition, treatment options, and lifestyle modifications for better self-management.

Example:

Research reputable sources, attend educational sessions, and ask questions during medical appointments.

8. Build a Support Network:

Tip:

Surround yourself with understanding individuals, join support groups, and communicate your needs.

Example:

Connect with friends, family members, or online communities for emotional support and shared experiences.

9. Practice Self-Care:

Tip:

Prioritize activities that bring you joy, relaxation, and fulfillment to maintain overall well-being.

Example:

Engage in hobbies like painting, gardening, reading, or taking leisurely walks to reduce stress and boost mood.

10. Stay Positive and Hopeful:

Tip:

Focus on the present moment, set realistic goals, and celebrate small victories along your health journey.

Example:

Practice gratitude, visualize positive outcomes, and maintain hope for a better tomorrow despite health challenges.

> "*By integrating these tips and examples into your daily life, you can effectively manage chronic illnesses and enhance your quality of life.*
> *Remember that self-care, a positive mindset, and proactive steps in self-management play key roles in coping with chronic conditions.*"

E. An ideal daily routine for a retired person:

Morning:

- Wake Up Early : Start your day early to make the most of the morning hours.
- Morning Routine: Begin with gentle stretches or a short walk to wake up your body.
- Breakfast: Enjoy a healthy breakfast with a balance of nutrients to fuel your day.
- Mindfulness Practice: Engage in mindfulness activities like meditation or deep breathing to set a positive tone for the day.
- Hobbies or Activities: Dedicate time to hobbies or activities you enjoy, such as reading, gardening, painting, or puzzles.

Mid-Morning:

- Social Interaction: Connect with friends or family members through phone calls, video chats, or social activities.
- Exercise: Engage in low-impact exercises like yoga, tai chi, or a morning stroll in the neighborhood.

Afternoon:

- Lunch: Have a well-balanced lunch with a focus on fresh vegetables, lean proteins, whole grains, and healthy fats.
- Rest and Relaxation: Take a short nap or engage in relaxing activities like listening to music or enjoying a good book.
- Personal Care: Attend to personal care tasks like grooming, skincare, or appointments if needed.

Late Afternoon:

- Outdoor Time: Spend time outdoors, perhaps tending to a garden, taking a leisurely walk, or sitting in a park to soak up some sunlight.
- Creative Pursuits: Engage in creative pursuits like painting, crafting, or writing to stimulate your mind.

Evening:

- Dinner Preparation: Prepare a light and nutritious dinner with a focus on whole foods and balanced portions.
- Dinner: Enjoy a family meal or dine with a partner to foster connections and conversation.

Evening Activities:

- Engage in leisurely activities like watching a movie, playing board games, or socializing with neighbors.

Night:

- Wind Down: Start winding down an hour before bedtime with calming activities like reading or listening to soft music.
- Bedtime Routine: Establish a bedtime routine to signal your body that it's time to rest.
- Quality Sleep: Aim for 7-9 hours of quality sleep to ensure rest and rejuvenation for the next day.

"This routine can be customized based on personal preferences, health needs, and interests.

It's important to maintain a balance between physical activity, mental stimulation, social interaction, and relaxation to support overall well-being in retirement."

Final Thoughts

Write a letter to your future self, reflecting on your hopes for the retirement journey ahead.

Conclusion

This workbook is a tool for your journey into retirement, focusing on resilience through spirituality.

By engaging in these exercises and reflections, you will cultivate a deeper understanding of yourself and your path forward.

Embrace this transition as an opportunity for growth, connection, and renewal.